deluded

first edition published february 29th 2024.

deluded - a guide to situationships
copyright © 2024 by isabella dorta

independently published by isabella dorta
www.isabelladortapoetry.com

paperback isbn: 978-1-7391789-2-5
ebook isbn: 978-1-7391789-3-2

primary editor: angela innes
secondary editor: zoë jellico
book cover artist: samantha sanderson-marshall
internal illustrator: laura martin

so to any exes reading this disclaimer,
if the shoe fits, i didn't put it on your foot.

ALSO BY ISABELLA DORTA

how sunflowers bloom under moonlight

how to be heartbroken

how to be mentally well

the letters i will never send

AVAILABLE FROM AMAZON & ALL MAJOR
RETAILERS.

CONTENTS

to cupid, my beloved kitten, who taught me more about love in his one little year of life than i expect anyone else ever will.

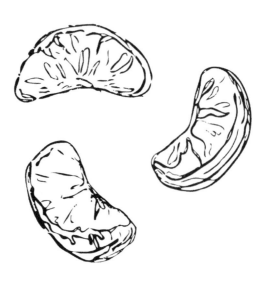

deluded

a guide to situationships

isabella dorta

i long to live in a house with large enough windows to climb
out of. i wish to sit upon the window sills and gaze out at
street lamps and quiet grass. i'd squeeze my body through
the frame just to smoke a cigarette or two and i would not
care in the slightest if i caught my clothes on a rusty, old nail.
a bad habit, yes, but oh how i know it would calm me on
nights like this, where my body feels too much like mine to
sleep comfortably in.

there are many evenings where i wish my body did not have
to belong to me. it would be easier, would it not? if someone
else could just take me, release me of this burden and let me
breathe without these ribs in the way. i am almost positive i
would be happier as a nothingness.

things would smell better
through any nose but mine,
taste sweeter
without my tastebud-bitten tongue,
look softer
through eyes born empty to pessimism.

and i am quite afraid that i have not learnt how to live
correctly yet.

but perhaps a windowsill may help; long, victorian panes of
glass and landlord painted, chipping ledges. an old home on a
road with overgrown curb corners and neighbours who
would never be caught awake past eight pm. i would quite
like somewhere to call my own, someplace mine and no one

else's, something that, for once, i am not afraid to crawl back
to.

the sky is a whole lot of nothingness, is it not? there are
pockets of aliveness, galaxies and stars and whatever else we
are yet to discover, but is it not the nothingness that serves as
the backdrop for these phenomenons?

would a star still be a star if it were not for the blackness
surrounding it?
would it still be as pretty?
as loved?
is my true desire to not exist
fuelled by my need
to make my loved ones shine?
i would fade into absolute darkness
if i knew it would benefit them.

and this is not selfless, i must remind you, i have not and
more than likely will not, ever be a good enough person to be
selfless. no, i expect i would destroy myself for them and still
make it about myself somehow, much like how we call the
sky 'the sky' and not the planets and stars.

but it would be glorious, would it not?

to be known in your death as a beacon of light for someone
you love, to fuel their desires for success, beauty, passions,
achievements?

i suppose, with all my heart's intentions, i must be frank and admit i have not uttered a single breath since beginning to write this. i have no window ledge, nor stars to make shine, i have only my childhood bedroom and this paper that i am writing to you on. i fear i may drown in my duvet one day, choking on ink, with my lungs full of half-written poems.

it is for the best. i cannot promise a windowsill-ed life would leave me any kinder to myself.

step 1

the before

there is a certain skill in delusion,

in burying your head into the sand,
or into the shoulder of whoever will let you.

it might not be art,
but it is damn near close-

to take a few, spared words as gospel
promises
and an unbothered body as a lover.

if that is not talent,
i do not know what is.

i've just been hurt so many times in the past,
i can't help but date pessimistically.
i don't want to.
i want to throw myself into love
and be passionate
and carefree
and enjoy how gentle skin feels

but i
can't.

i'm so afraid of being left by someone else,
and having to rebuild myself again and again,
it's exhausting.

i spend so much time worrying about
if they like me
and i barely even consider
if i like them.

i'm anxious when attached
and i'm scared of what happens when i'm not.
i don't mean to be demanding
or difficult
but i don't know how not to be anymore.

and another thousand love poems
will be written

and another thousand love poems
will go unread

and another poet
will wallow

and another muse
will be none the wiser.

because to be loved is to be seen, but to love is to be
invisible. to love is to be quiet and patient and lurking in the
shadows and wishing you were in the clouds. to love is to be
both blessed and cursed, to long for and pine after and pray
to and be given nothing in return. to love is to weep into your
pillow at night-time while your not-quite-lover sleeps
soundly on theirs. to love is to sacrifice yourself for the
greater good, to claw and gouge and breathe life into ink. to
love is to write and to hope that nobody will ever read it-

nobody except your muse.

when will it ever be my turn?
my chance to be kissed tenderly
and held in the evenings

and loved?
loved-

i just want to be loved!

i want someone to adore me
and kiss me
and touch me like there is not a single thing
their fingers would prefer to graze.

love me! please!

somebody.
just.
love.
me!

this life has been unkind and my heart has been rubbed raw.
the universe has not rewarded my goodness with more good.
oh, how i have begged.

the universe has laughed at me and informed me without
words that if i must expose my soft body, to ready myself to
be bitten and devoured.

and although my ears have remained closed and eyes have
remained tightly shut, my bones have listened. they have
understood this truth and this freight and they ache in
knowledge of how my vulnerability will be the death of me.

the universe has both
given
and
taken
too much from me.

i am undeserving of this body
and things that have been done to it.

if love is not supposed
to always be
so difficult,

why on earth have you
always found it
so difficult?

why has love never served itself
on a silver platter to you?

if love can be fun
and carefree
and simple,
why has love always felt like hard work?

if love could have come easy,
why has it
never
come easy to you?

is it love's fault?
or yours?

i am so afraid of life,

i am living
like i have already died.

i am alone,
i am the other woman
and i will never,
ever
learn.

i will think these men like me,
that they mean it when they say
they want to be my friend.

i will believe it when they tell me
how different i am to their girlfriends
and i will be happy to hear
about what they wish they could do to me.

i am pathetic. worthless. a bad feminist.

i hate myself for always falling for it.

i don't think you're very happy right now.

i think you pretend to be.
i think you tell everyone in your life
that you're fine

but i know that when you get home at night,
when you lock that bathroom door
and stare into that mirror
all you see
is a very, very sad pair of eyes
staring back at you.

i think every time your head hits the pillow,
you think about everything you said that day
and everything you didn't say that day
and everything you should've said that day
and i think you hate yourself for it.

i think you hate yourself for who you are
and who you're not.
i think you wish you were somehow
everyone else
and no one
all at once.

i think you know you're a shell of yourself
and i think you're afraid
for what that means.
you don't want to go through
the years of therapy again.
the antidepressants,
the trips to the doctors,

the pity stares,
having to explain to your family
that you're not doing okay again.

so i think you're just pretending.

i think you're putting on a brave face
and telling all of your friends
that you're fine,
but i think you know deep down that you're not.

i wish i could make it easier for you
but i can't.

i know that it's hard to admit,
but you have to,
because it's the first step in getting better.
you have to tell yourself
you're not happy.
you have to stop pretending.
you have to be honest with yourself
and everyone around you.
you have to tell them that you're struggling.
because you are,
aren't you?

you're struggling.

deluded- a guide to situationships

is there something wrong with me
or has love
just forgotten about me?

am i at the bottom of her list?
not memorable enough
to be plucked
from a crowd
and rewarded with
affection-

am i too boring to be loved?

i am predictably difficult and assuming and untrusting and
uncertainty has always been something i am good at.

i can ask you a million questions
and change my mind a million times over
before you have ever even uttered
a single answer.

i cannot be consistent for the life of me.
i am either thirty minutes late, or thirty minutes early
and no matter what time i arrive,
i will still hate myself for how i enter every room.

i do not want to be like this,
i do not want to be so unsure of myself
or despise myself as much as i do,
but i can't seem to stop.

i am the girl you long to fuck,

the one you cant wait to brag to your friends about,
the one who's hand you hold in public
because you want every stranger who walks past
to see that you managed to convince me
to spend my evening
with you.

i am the trophy,
the thing you want to own.
i'm not the girl who's face you hold tenderly
when were alone in bed together,
who you whisper sweet nothings to,
who you text at the end of every day.

i'm just the girl you want to fuck.
because that's all i'll ever be to men like you,
just a warm body you want to lay between.
you have no desire to understand
what's underneath my skin.

'love will come to you when you stop looking for it.'

'love is always best when it is the least expected.'

'love will find you, you won't find it.'

fuck. off.

love will not come to me from nowhere. love will not spring up out of thin air and surprise me with it's presence. love is not going to shake me awake and stop me from this nightmare. love is never going to find me.

so stop telling me that it will. it only hurts more to have to disappoint you and tell you that love has not come for me yet. i am sick enough as it is without having to accept pity stares and reassuring arm rubs. being single will not kill me. yes, of course i would far rather find my soulmate than spend the rest of my life alone, but i do not think i am the sort of person who is lucky enough to be given that opportunity.

if i was though, if by some chance love did find me, while i was walking the dog, or buying oat milk, or out dancing one evening, if love did tap me on my shoulder and force me to stop in my tracks, i would never let love go.

i would dig my nails into love, i would rip everything apart just to keep hold. i would love love, with everything in me and i would hope that love would do the same.

my name is not called,
my face is not kissed,
my hands are not held.

i am the last in line,
still waiting to be asked to dance,

still not picked
for the dodgeball team,
even though,
i swear to god!
i am filled
with enough rage to hit a girl called stacey,
with perfect hair and perfect teeth,
right in the throat with an illegal throw.

i'm kidding...
a little bit.

i am standing on the edge of the plank
and not a single hot pirate
has come to rescue me,
no fugitive is climbing up the side of my tower,
no pretty prince praying for me
to prick my finger
on a spinning wheel.

no one
cares.

no one wants me.
there is no one asking
to save me,

but i'm here,
distressed,
acting a damsel
and swiping right
endlessly on tinder,

hoping and praying and pleading
that one day,
one day soon,
someone
will come for me.

beyond this house, there is uncomfortable air.
heavy and hot and
busy.

there are people jostling and thriving and dying
and i want no part in
any of it.

i am peering out the window
and i like it here.
it is safe.
and quiet.
i want to stay inside and be alone
and not have to worry about another human being
for as long as i can.

and obviously,
i also do not want any of that.

i want to love and be loved
and have problems like
being late for the bus.
i want to breathe, fully,
until my lungs burst with summer breeze.
i want to get stuck in crowds
and stand shoulder to shoulder with strangers,
so close we can taste each others perfume.

i want to live,
loudly,
spend all my time outdoors
and drink pints in the winter in pub gardens
and freeze my fingers silly.

i want to eat oranges peeled by my lover
and never have to pick the rind out from
under my nails
ever again.

i want to stop collecting house plants
and grow wildflowers in my garden,
only watch movies in cinemas
and miss the most important parts,
because i ordered far too large of a diet coke
for my bladder to handle.

i want to do all the basic, boring, human bullshit
that everyone is always
complaining about.

and then i want to lay on my deathbed,
hold someone i love's hand
as i pass,
and i want to think about
how glad i am
that i lived.

love
is just around the corner.

it is so close,
we can almost smell it;

we know the way it will feel for our
bodies to crawl home.

love is not quite yet
within arms reach

and so

we are outstretched
and spinning,

ready
for her.

love
is the next season

and the next month
and the next tomorrow.

praise me for my devotion to the god of
love.

look at how i have begged,

see my palms bruised
and calloused
and then
tell me i have not begged enough.

i will die praying before i die alone.

i will long for love until the longing kills me.

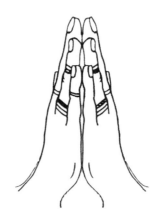

i want to meet men
so kind,
that i understand
why women decide
to hyphenate their
last name.

and i want a husband
so kind,
that my daughter becomes
one of these
women.

and it is not just love that i want.

it is less hurt.
less coldness.
less nothing.

it is not just love that i am hungry for,
i know that i cannot survive
on a diet of just kisses alone.

i want the lazy sunday mornings
that turn into lazy sunday lunches
that turn into lazy sundays evenings.

and then i'd quite enjoy a lazy monday morning,
one where we both call in sick to work
just to lie in bed next to one another
for as long as we can manage.

i want to kiss you
with a mouth full of morning breath
and night-time angst.
because eight hours is far too long
to go without laying your lips
onto mine.

and perhaps this is more than love
that i am asking for.

perhaps i am being greedy
when i ask the universe
to bless me with all of this,

but, my lord,

if i do not ask,
if i do not speak these desires into existence,
what is the point in owning a tongue?

what is the point
in being given the pleasure
of begging for love,
if i do not use it
and beg
at every given opportunity?

why would i waste a single second
not?

it must come for me soon,
that feeling in chests that hurts and speaks in tongues
and bites it's way out.
i want earthquakes in my bones
and numb feet
and hands so warm, i cannot feel my own skin.
i want to pull my own hair out,
clawing at the idea of love that lives in my brain,
my fingers will do anything
to touch,
to be closer
to hold that love in the very centre of my palms.

i am exhausted and exhausted and exhausted and
i want to be
so full of love,
that i am nauseous.

love is
slow.
love is
dragging her feet.
love is
quiet and angry and frustratingly unexplainable.

love is expected to be fast, though, isn't she? love is force-
fed to us as impulsive and quick and we watch how she fills
our screens before we can even speak her name. love is
described as all around us, but just out of arms reach, waiting
behind the next street corner, hiding underneath the mattress.
love is everywhere and nowhere all at once and it is. fucking.
annoying. having love is not the same as being loved and
they do not care at all if they do not come together; there is
nothing stopping love from abandoning you in the middle of
the night and this is why she is fleeting.

love is never there when you want her to be. she is evasive
and annoying and seems to belong to everyone except us,
doesn't she? love will tell you she is the best thing that could
ever happen to you, and then she will decide to just never
happen. love is unpredictable and dangerous and daring and i
have never hated anything more.

i hate love,

and i don't.

love is clawing at my feet and begging for acknowledgement.
love has said she is kind and good and as misconstrued as i
am. love has asked me to be patient and to wait for her and to
not twiddle my thumbs in the process. love has asked me not
to listen to what is said about her, to not pay attention to how
she is tarnished by her older sister, lust. she says she has
shown me, time and time again, how she plans to surprise me
gently.

love tastes like an easy sunday morning, with breakfast in
bed and a freshly squeezed glass of orange juice.
love is both my enemy and my longest friend. love is
everything i have ever wanted and nothing i have ever had.

love is
slow.
oh how i wish she wasn't.

i don't imagine love to be
knackering.

i imagine love to feel like
rest.

but if i am not hopeful, what is the point of living?
if i do not wake with dreams bigger
than the day before,
if i am not always ready and waiting
for it to be my turn,
why keep on going
if i am not excited for tomorrow?

i have to stay wishful.
i have to know
that the universe has a plan for me.

and perhaps not every single thing
must happen for a reason,
and perhaps not every bad thing
that has happened to me was deserved,
but how comforting it is to know that

everything i could ever think about wanting
is possible.
and everyone i could ever think about loving
is waiting for me to find them.

step 2

the beginning

and maybe the stories are true.
maybe i have had it wrong all along.
maybe this love nonsense is
as unpredictable as everyone says it is.

because you came out of nowhere.
you just sprung up out of thin air and you

took notice of me.

and oh, it feels
lovely.

new is scary.
new is uncomfortable.
new is not always welcomed.

new is the barista in your usual coffee shop
messing up your drink order
and being forced to try out almond milk
for the first time,
and liking it more than oat.

new is buying the next size up
in the same pair of jeans
you've worn since you were fifteen.
and crying in the changing rooms
for embarrassingly long.

new is going vegan this january,
but just for the month,
and accidentally staying vegan for february.
and march.
and april.
and may.

new is a boyfriend buying you
your ex's favourite flowers
and you know they're not quite new,
but they feel it.

new is missing your stop on a train
because you fell asleep daydreaming,
and staring out of the window of the taxi
the entire way home,
vowing to move cities one day soon.

new is a first date
that you're really not sure you even want to go on
but you do,
because maybe new doesn't have to be scary
or uncomfortable
or not always welcome.

and maybe the dinner goes well,
and your date makes you laugh
and you walk home,
with your headphones in,
singing to yourself
in a way that only
people in love
can.

first dates have never been my forte,
i am a little bit awkward
and weird
and i'm really only funny
when no one is paying attention.

but for you,
i want to be good at them.

i want to be confident and easygoing and
the sort of girl who orders something fancy,
like a manhattan
or a martini, extra dry.

but i don't really understand what makes a drink dry,
and i can't pretend i didn't change outfits three times
before finally leaving the house,
and i am definitely far too anxious to,
in any way shape of form,
come across as anything other than
a nervous wreck.

i am nail biting, leg bouncing, eye twitching
and i will probably forget to breathe
at least twice.

i hope you don't mind.
i so hope you're nice.

i hope this make-up

will make you like me
more,

will make you want to love me
more.

do my cheeks seen more kissable this rosy?
do my lips feel better outlined and painted?
do my eyes look prettier smudged with black for
your pleasure?

i am a sheep in wolf's clothing
and i hope you will not see right through me.

i stand in front of the mirror,
lips parted,
eyes wide open,
holding a mascara wand that's about
three centimetres away from blinding me.

i hope he thinks i look pretty tonight.

i'm desperate to please him,
to make him fall in love with me instantaneously
when he sees me tonight.
i've been starving myself for the last week.
in all honesty, i was afraid he would think
there was too much of me to love.

he told me over text that he likes it
when women wear their hair tied back
and so i gel each baby hair flat against my scalp,
even though i know
it'll look like shit tomorrow morning,
especially if i let him convince me to
spend the night in his bed.

i wear my highest heels,
because for some reason he just *loves* tall women.
and even though i have always dreamt of
a petite love, one that makes me feel
worthwhile and like a real woman
(because we all know small equals beautiful),
i know compromising is important in a relationship.

i cry twice while picking out what to wear
and end up in a ball on my bedroom floor

surrounded by dresses i bought as a teenager
and smudging the stupid mascara
i've always hated wearing.
i'm an embarrassment of a woman.

and then he texts me,
tells me he's just *so* excited to meet me,
but he can't get this bloody tie right,
and do i know what a windsor knot
is supposed to look like?
it is then that i know we are going to be
just fine.

dating is nerves and
self-doubt and
smudged mascara
that you wipe off with toilet paper,
and throw in the bin
on your way out of the door.

and then i saw you for the first time

and my heart did not stop.

and i was more alive than i have ever been.

and i liked it.

my hands are calm and your voice feels like honey in my ears and your eyes are so easy to look at.

this is not how it is supposed to go. this is too easy, too unremarkable. i should be in the toilets, anxiously texting my friends and having a nervous wee before sitting back down and ordering another drink, hoping this one will calm my nerves.

but i'm not.

i'm sat in front of you, looking at those pretty hazel eyes and i have forgotten that i ever even ordered this vodka coke. ice melts and my heart matches.

does he feel this too?
are his cheeks that red from me
or the cold?
is this
reciprocated?

finally,
for once,
for the first time in a really, really long fucking time,
does someone else want to be here as much as i do?

his eyes aren't quite meeting mine
and it could very well just be because he doesn't like
making eye contact,
but i can hear my heart screaming for me
to be
the cause.

his nerves make mine quieten
and although i can't be sure,
i think can see him staring at the blush on my face.

let us play footsie under the table,
bump knees and pretend we are oblivious to the static,
use thumbs to draw circles in palms.

trail your fingertips across the tops of my thighs
and i will let you watch me shiver.

touch starved,
hungry and
pink,
my skin has been yours
since it was formed in the womb.

i did not know it then,
i did not even know it yesterday,
but i know it now.

deluded- a guide to situationships

you bury your face into my neck
while i hug you goodbye.

you breathe me in,
moan at the citrus lining my collarbones,
and i think about how i will wear
only this perfume
for the rest of my life.

it is orange peel and cinnamon
and nervous sweat
and

you
like
it.

if my skin is to ever smell of
anything,
if i am to ever sweeten a nose
again,
i will not let it be with any
scent but this one.

i vow to buy out every bottle,
memorise every ingredient on the label,
go into debt just to feed this weakness.

you like it
and i like you
and we both like the smell of
oranges.

we do not kiss.
we linger for embarrassingly long.
we turn and walk away.

i look back.
you look back.

oh.

i think you like me
just as much as
i like you.

the first night i tried to sleep after i met you,
i failed,
horribly.

i tossed and turned
and replayed every look.
i lived the next thirty years with you in no more than
four
measly
hours.

and i longed for you to call,
or text,
or send me another like on another dating app
(or whatever it is normal people do
when they like somebody nowadays)

i wanted it-
you-
i wanted you.

and then out of nowhere,
sleep found me
as quickly as you did.
i woke up smiling,
pining,
more excited and present
than i ever thought i could be.

condensation lines my windows and i watch it race down the panes and i do not dare to try and go back to sleep. my pillow feels lumpier than usual and i wonder if i can afford a new set before remembering i am now poor in everything except love. and besides, nothing man-made could ever feel as good as my head did on your shoulder. something has sat on top of me, ripped holes in my ribcage, taken ahold of my heart and i hope it is your kind hands.

have me. as you wish. it has been mere hours and i am more sure of this than i have been of anything ever. i am more sure of you than i am of myself.

and if this is how loving you feels after such a short time, i can only assume spending years with you, would be nothing short of glorious. if i am to be called a fool, so be it- fool me. if i do not jump from this cliff, i fear i will be forever stuck in the clouds, and i would so rather prefer a life on solid ground with you. catch me as i fall, fall with me, meet me at the bottom. let us shut our eyes and ignore the scenery on the way down. i care only about how you feel in my arms.

in this house, on this morning, with this love, i am invincible. and this is only the beginning,

i can feel it.

be sure of me.
surer.
know that this is an absolutely terrible idea
and do it anyway.
kiss me while everyone is watching,
hold onto me in public and love me loudly.

let the timing be wrong
always,
but let us chose each other anyway.

make it hard work,
near impossible work,
unachievable, unattainable work
and make us long to do it anyway.

this will not be an easy sunday morning kind of love,

this will be a monday evening,
sink full of dishes,
empty fridge,
no money for take out
kind of love.

a hill that you're really not sure ever ends kind of love
a favorite jumper in the wash kind of love
an incredibly inconvenient kind
of love

but
pick. me. anyway.

every morning,
pick me again.
choose me daily
and without pause or breath.
make bad decision after bad decision
and eventually let it all make sense.
let enough bad decisions turn into something worthwhile.

wake up next to me in three months time,
brush the sleep out of my eyes and the rattiness out of my
hair
and think

*'i cannot believe i ever thought this love
was a bad idea.'*

i'd like for you to kiss me now.

not softly,
or with caution,
just kiss me like you need me.

like ever since you first laid eyes on me,
it's all you've been thinking about.

like you cannot fall asleep
without imagining my lips
every
single
night.

kiss me like this is everything you've ever wanted,

like my lips hold the cure
to every disease
you could ever possibly have.

like my face is just-
just exactly
what you want.

kiss me
kindly,
but with passion and
gently,
but with this burning need.

kiss me with
everything you have
and i promise,
i will kiss you right back
with everything
i have.

please!
i'm so desperate
and it's so unattractive,
but oh my god
i want you.

i want you to kiss me so badly.

before you,
there was a string of men who hurt me,
who pretended to love me,
who, really, only wanted me for
that one little thing i try so hard not to think about.

i was not cared for.
i was not appreciated.

and maybe me telling you this
makes me too vulnerable,
maybe this leaves me weak
and at risk of history repeating itself,
maybe this gives you all the signs you need to know
that i am going to be easy to manipulate,

but i hope it won't.
i hope you will be kind.

i like your cupids bow
more than any other
i have ever seen
and i am still yet to
feel it.

deluded- a guide to situationships

i am driving,
i am singing badly to taylor swift
and there has not been a single red light in the last fifteen
minutes.

the sun has decided to show her purples to the world
and my windows have rolled themselves all the way down.

but,
and this is unfortunate,

i cannot think of anything other
than the curls on the
nape of your neck.

this is, of course, why my singing is so bad.

it is hard to stay on pitch when you have littered
every corner of my mind
with the three rings
you wear on your fingers.

i can smell your aftershave on the collar of my shirt still
and it takes everything in me
not to close my eyes
every time i inhale.

i feel your palms on my shoulder blades-
delicate and careful and purposeful
but afraid.

i like how you touch me.

it is gentler than i'm used to,
your fingertips
do not dig themselves into my flesh
like they are pleading to leave their mark
in invisible bruises
that spell
'i was here'
to every man that comes after you.

you are the first man
who has not wanted me
to be branded
by you.

my flower print pillow cases-
propped up on elbows and shaking wrists.
our foreheads pressed,
bare skin barely touching.

i pull away
just to stare at you
a little
better.

we do not move,
not even a flinch of a smile,
but i know we are both smiling.
time has never existed before this moment
and i am not sure it ever will again.

i could spend an eternity here-
right here.
with you.

with.
just.
you.

look at me like that again,
oh please, i beg,
look at me like you may possess the desire
to love me.

it was fleeting, curled up in my bedsheets,
but it was there.
i cannot sleep without remembering of it.

you are uncomfortable.
fidgeting and
fleeting and
planning
how you will exit my life
already,
even though
you have only just
arrived.

you are immaculate.
and i do not think you know of it yet,
but i do.

i see right through you,
down to the bone,
clean cut and white and
perfectly flawed.
i see what you have been trying to hide
with your flesh
and i like it.

you are not mine to own,
but
my oh my
how i crave you.

and i know i cannot have
all of you yet,
but,
daily,
i pray for our hands to meet.

you make me want to become religious,
so that i may have

someone but you
to beg to,

someone but you
to worship.

deluded- a guide to situationships

i know that you are more than likely
not the person
i have fallen in love with every night,
in whispers of dreams
and when late night imaginations
are left to run wild,
but it is not your fault
that you are not what i have imagined you to be.

you are probably flawed and difficult and

human.

i expect you shout just as much as the rest of us,
burn your toast in the mornings,
preoccupied and pondering life.
you probably leave nail clippings in the bathroom and
toothpaste stains lining the sink.

you probably do not shower every day
or clean your teeth religiously, like you should.
you are more than likely
a little bit
gross
and weird
and just
like
the rest of us.

the point is,

i want you
regardless of the fact that i do not know you

(yet),
in spite of not knowing you
(yet),
i want you more because
i do not know you.
i do not know who you are in conflict,
or in love.

i want to learn and study you
and take tests on how to touch you.

i have given you my heart
without ever knowing
the shape
or weight
of yours.

i do not know you,
yet,
and i want to.

teach me patience.
make my hands wait and hover over you,
let me breathe before i touch your skin with mine.
the tips of my fingers are hitting the keys on my laptop and
they are
screaming
for you. loudly.
oh how i can hear my heart beating in my ears,
this desire is deafening.

i would love the hell out of you.
i would.

i'd add oranges to my weekly shop because the smell
reminds me of meeting you and i'd swap my generic
toothpaste for the brand you like. i'd learn to wake up early,
make our bed every morning and if you told me you like
coffee, i'd memorize just how you like it.

i'd be your warmth after a cold day and i'd listen to you
complain about everyone who isn't me. i'd watch your
favorite shows and eat your favorite foods and read your
favorite books. i'd buy blankets in your favorite color just so
that i could sleep with some part of you on nights where your
absence is too loud.

i'd do the whole damn thing. i'd cut my hair just how you
like and i'd never wear odd socks in your presence ever
again. i'd shower in water as cold as you'd like because i'd
love you too much to change the settings from yours.

i'd do it all for you, whatever you asked of me (and then
probably some more just for good measure). i'd place not a
single foot out of line, nor would i ignore a single skipped
beat from my heart.

i'd remember everything that you love and i'd hope that this
would mean that i would never need to be reminded of who i
am again. i'd lose myself to your love and i would find
myself again every night in your arms. i-

i'd squeeze you fresh orange juice every morning, gag at
peppermint toothpaste, become an early bird who still

somehow always misses the worm and swap my tea for your coffee. i'd forget i own vocal chords, love everything that you love, become everything you could love and never touch hot water again for as long as i live.

i'd bloody myself in the process of loving you. grazed knees from praying on my bedroom floor for your happiness and bruised palms from practicing how i will hold yours.

i. would. love. the. hell. out. of. you.
i would.

look inside my heart and see the way my blood pools in
curves that scream your name,
carve out each syllable and do not be gentle and

make
me
bleed.

spell me silly-
i need not know of more than your four letters
for as long as i beat.
this heart is pointless
if it is not obvious to everybody else
that it is yours.

own
me.

use
me.

just.
have.
me-

exactly as i come.

do not ask me to change or mold myself to your hands.
i will,
but do not ask for it.
let me alter myself willingly,
disfigure my body with love and worship.
let me,

deluded- a guide to situationships

over many years,
wear down my kneecaps
into dust from praying on your bedroom floor
in front of you.

i wish for necessary hip replacements
from trying to match your strides
and fillings from tooth decay
because i refuse to leave your bed in the mornings.
give me broken fingernails
from clawing onto this gorgeous love
and ripped out hair follicles
so that i can soften my body
against yours.

i will gladly destroy myself loving you.
i have no shame
in how i will make this body ache
for you,

daring and
careless and
with my stomach in my mouth,
i will adore you.
daily.

and,
after the sacrifices
have been made
and the body
has been ruined,
i will be nothing
but a heart,

but a bloody mess
with your name carved in.

you will not love me
once you see what i have done to myself
and i will only love you more for it.

the way you have standards that i do not fit into will turn me into
a quivering mess.
you will hate me almost as much as i do.

oh how that excites me.

and if this is love, then so be it. let me buy extra cleaning cloths for the crumbs your toast makes and hoover head attachments for your bathroom beard trimming messes. let me love you from afar, from close by, from the outside in and the inside out. let me savour not a single thing as sweet as your touch for as long as i live, my tastebuds would rather starve than not know your own. i swear, i have never known my fingers to write as fast of anyone as they do of you. they are skipping over the keys, drunk and deliciously delirious. you have infested not only my heart, but every inch of my skin, and with every tap of my fingertips on my keyboard, i can feel you being embedded even further into me. i am overrun with love for you and i do not dare to mind it. oh how human you make me feel.

step 3

the longing

i really think i do love them.

i wasn't so sure for a while, i thought i might, but if i'm honest, the thought absolutely petrified me, so i pushed it right down and did my best to forget about it. it makes me so sad really- when i picture falling in love, i think of exciting newness and spring and everything that is almost brilliance. i didn't grow up imagining i'd be too afraid to let myself go, all i had ever wanted was to throw all my caution to the wind and let myself fall into this gooey love that i couldn't climb out of. i think in theory, this is so much easier than it is in practice.

but i am stuck.

i have unfortunately had the wind knocked out of me and my god, for the first time in a very, very long time, i can finally feel the butterflies in my stomach properly again. i am very much in love with them.

dramatic,
aren't i?

i'm dramatic in the way that i love you,
how i grab onto your face
every time you kiss me,
god, i act as if we're in some
stupid romcom.

i hold onto your hand in public,
your thigh under the table.
i love you loudly and unapologetically and dramatically.
i know i do.

i think you like it though.
 a little bit,
right?

no one has ever loved you
like this before.
no one has ever kissed
every inch of your body
and told you how beautiful you are.

no one
has ever bought you
flowers.

i love buying you flowers,
maybe it's just
me being dramatic
but the way your face
lights up

when you receive them
makes everything so worthwhile.

i swear, i'd spend my entire salary
on flowers
if it meant i got to see you smile
as wide as you did
that first time

dramatic,
aren't i?
yeah,
maybe,
but i'm in love so
there are worse things i could be.

oh i cannot help but pry my ribcage apart for you.
i would like my body to be as comfortable as possible
for you to lay your head upon.
if i must lose bones for your skull, i will.
rip me limb from limb,
take parts of me as souvenirs, keyrings and postcards.
scatter me,
do with me as you please,
give me a purpose to my destroying.
let it be for love.

i am so disappointingly loving.
louder than i can shout,
my heart has beaten for you
from our first meet.

i wish for your ears to hear how i speak of you when you are not around. i beg of you to hover in the doorway of every room i inhabit, place every glass you own against every wall i have. eavesdrop on me shamelessly. i am not brave enough to tell you of how i love you, but i cannot stop myself from telling every stranger i meet of your kindness. you must know you have the only name my mouth enjoys saying.

i don't think love is a burden.

i am not tired
of having my
arms wrapped around you,
my face held by you-

you are not boring me.
you are everything to me.

i am yours and yours and yours some more.

is it normal to love this quickly? to fall so utterly head over heels? oh darling, my darling, you have me in the very palm of your hand. your voice and my spine dance with one another, my lips long for yours and my eyes cannot rest in the evenings, unless it is you they see last. i have known you for far less time than i have known myself but in these short few months, your love has taught me how to love myself again. i have not done this since i was a child.

do you see how my spine curves for you?
my thighs dimple in a morse code that calls your name.
baby-
my collarbones are yours.
own my skin and caress me as gently as you please.
i only ask for your kind body in return.

and every other fruit is tasteless

and every other person is boring

and i'd like to peel oranges with you like we did
once before

and i want to feel the juice run down my wrists

and if you want to lick my palms clean,
that would be nice

and you should let me feed you each segment

and then we should kiss so hard,
that later when i shower,

i find citrus in my hair.

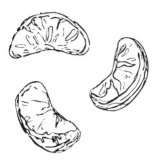

you make me want to hold breath in fear of startling your
hands from around my waist.

i know i have lived before you, i know i have not always
needed help containing my organs to my body, but the
second you remove your hands i worry i may spill onto you
in a way i cannot control.

my blood is clumsy and my heart cannot help
but match.

i sleep with
fingers on collarbones
and flowers on my pillowcase
and wake to water running down my windows.

once-
under candlelight, a cold duvet and a comforter,
you placed me in the crook of your shoulder
and stopped my body from shaking as i sobbed.

and whilst i have often found myself
weeping in the arms
of the men that i have loved,
not once have they held me back.

oh, this…
is the most i have ever been
loved.

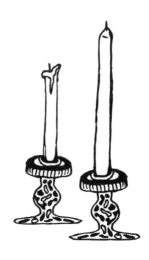

to watch your hands
sit around my hips
like i am
drinkable liquid,

cup me.

this skin is warming your palms
until they are
as alive
as this love is.

this is everything.

we are giggling like school children
and breathless like teenagers
and i love you like i have grown old with you already.

share breaths with me,
baby.

gasp into my mouth as i touch you,
be wordless,
be eyes rolled to the back of your head in pleasure,
be mine.
in this very moment,
let me own you with my fingertips.
i want to graze all of you-

delicate,
aren't you,
baby?

your lips sweet and the inside of your thighs soft,
my mouth is perfect only for kissing you.
oh and your hipbones,
glorious.

i could sip wine from your collar bones once
and never need to drink a single thing,
ever again.
you taste like everything i have ever craved

thank you, baby,
this pleasure is unmatched.

you are magic,
you know?
patient and
sweet-natured and
gorgeous.

you're the sort of man
i would be stupid not to love.
you're the sort of man
any person would be stupid not to love.

you hold me gently
and like you want me but never like you need me.
i have never been made to feel demanded by you.

i am a choice,
not just a thing you need,
not an obligation
or a requirement,
but a choice.

i am desired
and cared for
and kissed
and touched
and praised
and hugged
and looked at
and maybe
almost

loved.

he cooks my favourite meal,
does not let me set the table,
stir the pot
or wash the dishes after.

instead,
he lifts me up
onto the kitchen counter,
bubbles still dripping from his forearms
while he holds me.

domestic bliss has never quite made sense to me
before this man came into my life.
now,
i refuse to ever accept anything less.

sweet touches, *please.*
need i remind you to use only the pads
of your fingers?
cup me and drink all of me.
use your thumb to skim the surface.

your hand has found my face
a thousand times over
and yet,
every time,
i feel my heart rise up into my head
to meet it
as if it is the first.

oh how you continue to move me.

i suppose,
if i'm honest,
it is not always perfect.

i do sometimes lie to my friends
when they ask how it is going.

i don't tell them about the girl at the bar
i saw him talking to,
or how he broke a dinner plate last week
after i didn't slice the carrots
how he likes me to.

i don't want them to worry,
and there's nothing to worry about anyway,
right?

it's okay if i love him
more than he loves me,

this love is normal,

right?

is this a relationship, or have i convinced myself that these late night hangouts are love when they are not?

am i wrong to love you? to hold everything in my chest and feel like i am bursting at the seams? do you lay next to me after i give you all that pleasure and fantasise about a long life with me? do you see me and want to cry, like i do with you?

i know you don't. deep down. i know this is a one-sided love. i write fictional poem after fictional poem and i try to use these silly words to turn what we have into something more. i don't think it's working.

i suppose i cannot help but hope that if i continue to love you, if i continue to write for you, if i am the best fuck i can possibly be for you, maybe that love will grow for you too. maybe you will decide you cannot do anything but love me and maybe you will tell me finally, everything i have been waiting to hear.

ignore every red flag.
forget that they have ever hurt you.
pretend this love has always been perfect.

kid yourself
into thinking they care.

this is a relationship if you dream hard enough.

and boy,
am i dreaming.

step 4

the delusion

lay next to me,
palms grazing skin
that has not been touched in months,
tell me that kissing me might just be
too romantic
for you,
before you place my fingers
over your
thighs.

i crave both softness and your beard stubble
on my cheek
and my entire existence
is a juxtaposition and
this
is why
you like me.

because
you do like me,

don't you?

you do not want to kiss me
or hold me before midnight
or trace the three freckles under my left eye
with your thumb
and

you only want to touch me when i am unclothed
or when the lights are dimmed
but

you do like me,

don't you?

you do think of me in my absence
and wonder how my morning is going,

don't you?

you read your books
and swap my name
with the pretty little love interest's,
daydream of doing the washing up with me,
walk past supermarket sushi counters
and remember my name,

don't you?

you do think about how you
laid next to me,

don't you?

if i am not enough for you,
do not tell me.
cheat or leave or do whatever men do
that allows women to hate them but
do not let me know
of this truth.

let me live in unhappy delusion,
i would rather hate you for leaving unexpectedly,
than hate myself
for being the reason you must leave me.

find the wings
tucked under
my shirt
and then cut them
from me.

ruin every hope
and every dream,

bind me to this earth.
let me not think of any
future i should have
held,

cover me
in cold iron
and watch on
as i suffer.

bring me nothing but
pain,
misfortune,
sheer misery.

destroy every last shred
of enjoyment
i may receive from this life
and force me to live it anyway.

torture me if you must.
i am sure we will both find
some pleasure in it.

sex is so far from what i want from you,
but god, i would let you fuck me senseless
if it would make you like me more.

i don't really even like sex,
it's sort of painful, if i'm honest,
and it always makes me want to sob after,

but then again,
the idea of having to exist without you
is more painful than any emotion i think i could ever feel.

so please,
kindly,
i offer you my body.

use as desired,
fold when needed,
rough or gentle,

i am a slave to the love you may offer.

dip my head underneath this cold.
let everything smell of salt and tulips and a blue
that is actually purple.

towel me dry with poetry-
lovely, warming poetry.
i am waiting.

i am waiting.

this can only ever be sin,
to lust as if we are dying,
to beg for skin like it is water.
and,
carelessly,
i have never felt more alive.

my body has never felt more
like mine than it does
when i am giving it to you.

devoid me of any
aloneness
i may ever feel.

ruin every quiet moment
and
spoil every second of peace i ask for.

let me not exist in silence ever
again.

hold my jawbone like it is gentle luck.
your thumb hot,
i can almost feel our skin fusing together at the corner of my
mouth.

wishful thinking perhaps, yes-
but if your fingers are not birthday candles,
dripping wax and hope,
then what are they?

fingers?!

do not lie to me,
you must feel this too.

you touch me
and you must know your hand belongs there.

promise me
you will not remove it
while i am conscious.

let me sleep happy before i wake alone.

it is inappropriate
how often i think of you.

it is appalling,
really.

day-ending,
mind-numbing,

heart
wrenching,

it is ridiculous.
i have only myself to blame,

but i cannot even seem
to find the time to do that.

and here is a promise-

i will love us
into the
ground.

breathe.

nobody will watch.
no fingers will be peaked through
nor pearls clutched in doorways,
gossip columns
or nosey neighbours.
it will be over
before a single person has acknowledged
it's beginning.

breathe.

it will be fast.
you will barely feel anything.
my dear,
my body will cushion yours
and take all of this silly pain
as only my own.
my hands will take yours
and you will not hear
of how i break
my own bones
to hold you.

breathe.

you will enjoy it,
for it's split-second-ness,
for it's momentary brilliance.
you will find it
shamefully romantic
how quickly
love
can turn into
boredom.

breathe.

i am fond of you-
fonder than i'd like to admit.

your back holds secrets my fingers beg to draw out.
let me trace everything i cannot say to you,
on you.
barely touching,
electricity born between us,
the pads of my fingers are too soft for their own good.

i.
want.
you.

every inch of my skin craves
every inch of yours.
and with the most respect that i can muster,
it is not sex i want from you.
i am not asking for anything other
than the pleasures
of feeling your back with my hands.

this is a love beyond words,
only containable by touch.
let me show you how well
i love you,
without ever having to say
a single thought,
in my silly little
love-struck brain.

deluded- a guide to situationships

i wrote of you,
like you asked.

i find it strange
that you have not realised already
that it is not as beautiful
as it first sounds
to be transcribed.

you are a muse
who has not quite yet seen the ugly
in your artist,

but you will.
you will.

it is not an honour
to be written of,
nor is it special
or fulfilling
or lovely.

in years to come,
this version of you will be gone,
all but for this
paper,

and that may sound exciting
but it is danger
wrapped in selfish, self preservation.

you will hate me
and the words

that came along with it all.

in this moment,
my love has been told to the world-
if the reader closes this book
on this exact page
and does not read on,
our love has never ended for them.

you think this is something
that will make future you happy?

you are daft.
you will grow to hate it.

my bones yearn for you.
hot, heavy sunlight,
you warm me.

let me lay myself flat on a rock in your way,
exposed soft spots
and vulnerable body,

kill me if you feel like it.
i am putty in your pleasant hands.

do you see how my body opens at your touch? how my ribs part themselves for your head and my fingers wrap around your own. i have pried myself in two for you, begged of you to sit comfortably in the middle and enclosed my silly little heart around you.

if they do not feel the same way, whether that be just yet or ever, i will cope. i think i will be okay. i want nothing more than to spend pretty much every waking moment i have free with them, and then some busy moments too. i want it to be me that they want, me that they see a future with, me that they want to spend all of their free time with.

but if it is not me, if i really have got it all wrong and when they see me, they feel stones in their chest and anxiety lining their spine, if they do not see love when they see my face, if it is not me, i hope whoever it is, finds them.

i hope they can leave me quietly and cherish this book of poems, even if it's only purpose served is to let them know how they deserve to be thought of. if this letter does nothing other than to help them to understand what they are plenty good enough for,

i will be grateful i was ever taught to write.

do you blame me?
for trying to mould myself into someone easier
for them to tolerate?
someone forgiving and meek,
do you hate me
for trying to make them love me?

have i disappointed you?
made you disgusted at the sight me?
do you wish i knew better?

i don't want to be pathetic.
i don't want to hold this much shame in my body.

but i am afraid of being alone.
and although they do not treat me nicely,
to me,

being mistreated is better than nothing at all.

must i remind you
of how it feels to hold my little body
in your arms?

i am weak and unmoving and damaged
and you like that.

i am worth saving, am i not?
most days, yes?

i am grateful to be loved, thanking you
with every full set of lungs i have,

every exhale
is the prayer
on my bedroom floor
that i make to you.

i am kneeling
until my knees give out
and then i pray laying down.

i am sorry and sorry and so sorry
i am undeserving of your love,
aren't i?

i beg and plead and ask for more forgiveness,
for a tighter hold,
for a small kiss on my shoulder.

i let you touch me
in every place
no person should touch,

deluded- a guide to situationships

each corner of my soul and
every fold of my brain and
each chamber of my heart.

your fingertips have prodded and bruised
and scratched your name deep into me.
i could not escape you if i tried.

must you forget that i belong to you?
must you decide
you do not want to own me any longer?

you have always liked my vulnerable state,
must i show you how broken i will be if you leave
for you to not?

must you leave?
must you?

step 5

the truth

and it hits me.

i will never be enough for you.

i will never have your babies or have you kneeling in front of me. i will never be good enough for you to love entirely. i will, from now and till forever, be nothing but a burden to you. nothing but a love sick puppy who you bought on a whim and decided was too much work a few months in. you have returned me back to sender, and packaged me up in whatever i came in, just a little less neatly and with a little more damage. you have asked for your time and money back, i was not a worthwhile investment.

you do not want me,
do you?
there is no warmth in your hands anymore.
i miss the sweetness that your voice used to carry
to the back of my throat.

once,
before you recognised my body for the carcass that it is,
you laid over me,
legs sprawled and arms folded.
i found peace inside of me that night.
having you use my body as a pillow

almost
made me
like it
again.

it is a shame that feeling did not last longer.

and with my hands,
i hold onto your shirt.

i hold on so hard,
it hurts.

my fingers are numb
and begging for more of you
and they
are as sore as my heart.

you have had all of me
(always),
since the moment you met me.
and in this very second
(and in all the seconds before this),
i have only
the material on your
chest.

this is how i plead of you to stay.
this is how i tell you i love you.
this is how you leave me.

pried fingers
and clenched fists
and a face so wet,
i cannot see you leave.

in a room so filled
with summer,
i have never felt
so cold.

deluded- a guide to situationships

there is sun
on every corner of my
bedsheet,
the cotton is warmed
with your body heat

and bunches of flowers
that i had to buy for myself
have dried,
while hung from my ceiling.

nothing can be smelt but my premature grief of you.

i know i will mourn you
for as long as i can love,
and then some more.
probably.

you're stupid, you know?
thinking they loved you back-

they didn't.
they still don't.

you pined after a person
who thinks you are
ridiculous.

and deep down you know it too.
you know you look ridiculous.

you're just
too scared
to admit it to yourself.

deluded- a guide to situationships

i really miss you.

and i know this is
really silly

because i also know that
you don't miss me back.

you aren't thinking about me in the slightest
but i just can't seem to stop myself tonight.

you're everything i hate
and you give me nothing that i need,

but all i want, is to watch you
sleep next to me.

it is taking everything in me
not to reach out to you,

i know i will only be met with silence
and small talk anyway,

but believe me,
i am counting down the days until i can see you again.

do you feel bad about hurting me?
do you regret it?

do you lay awake at night
and think about how you would've done it all differently
and not broken my heart?

because i lay in bed
and i think about what i could've done differently
to stop you from breaking my heart,
i think about how i could've loved you more
or less
because maybe me loving you too much
was the problem.

i think about how i could've acted differently,
allowed you to get away with more,
picked less fights,
started less arguments,

because even though you were the one
that was doing things to hurt me,
i still feel like i am to blame.
i still feel like it's my fault that you hurt me.

do you feel like that?
do you feel bad about hurting me?

all i ever wanted,
was to be the person
you'd turn around for.

the person
you'd fight for.

i know i do not have the perfect body,
or face,
my looks
are not the sort that men
fawn over.

i'm average,
a five out of ten
on a good day,

the sort of girl you could walk past
on the street,
every morning
on your way to work
and not even
notice.

i could serve you a coffee,
every morning
and i'd doubt you'd even
glance down
at my name tag.

i am invisible
to men like you,
just another thing
that isn't attractive enough
for you to take interest in.

i don't think you ever even looked at me
properly.

but as average as i may be,
as unremarkable
as i know you found me,
i have never loved you
with anything other
than all of me.

i was average
in everything except
my love
for you.

and i spend my evenings
missing you-

praying for your return
to be sped up,
or to just
happen
at all.

knowing that you might never come back to me
is torture,

i either want you gone forever
or here immediately.

i vow to ruin every wedding you have
that isn't to me.
i'll speak up
every time one of my friend's
pollute your name
every time someone says
how terrible you were to me,

i will defend you to god
if it is your mistreatment of me
that will not let you into heaven,
if it may help you be viewed as a little bit less
of a bad person.

i will contain myself
to the left hand side of every bed
i sleep in,
always,
empty or not.

i've never really been in love
but when you left,
i was not allowed to be alone for weeks.
i was not allowed to cut up my own fruit
or shower with the door closed
or have my phone unsupervised.

you've never been in love,
you reminded me of that often.

and i'm not stupid enough
to fall in love
with somebody

who didn't love me back.
so i've never
been in love,
right?

not seriously?
right?
can you just
give me this one thing
and let me pretend i have never,

never
loved
you.
please.

you look ridiculous,
pining after that man,
like he still loves you,
everyone hates him,
your family,
your friends,
his family and his friends
hate him too,
because that's how bad he was.
even they took your side.
and you still love him?
you're stupid.

i find love so incredibly hard.
i try so hard to not let myself find love.
i have spent too long broken
and in pain
and thinking i was ruined,
or damaged goods;

i don't think i am the sort of person
who could ever be
loved.

i know i am kind and smart
and my eyes sometimes look quite nice in sunlight,
but none of that
is enough,
none of that
has ever made anyone desperate for me.

and i think that's the crux of it all really-
all i have ever been
is convenient,
a time passer,

there when nothing better was around
to take
my place.

fifty-eight days.

there are fifty-eight days
between tonight
and when i may see you next.

fifty. eight. fucking. days.

oh and it is so not long enough.
i long for a number
too high for me to count,
one that is so large,
it might as well be final.

i cannot imagine how sweet healing would be
if i knew i would
never
have to see you again.

believe me when i tell you that i did not ask for this.

i have never been proud to love in the way that i do. there were too many colors to count on your face and i fear i may have underestimated the hold you had over me.

i did not warn you. i did not prepare you for the burden i was about to become. i am sorry, this poem is my late notice.

you dared to take my hand, and now, i will most likely feel your touch for the next ten years. and this is not an exaggeration, i can still recall the hand of the boy i fell in love with at thirteen. his were far less calloused than yours, less full of life and happiness. your hands always looked like they might remind me of spring. pleasant excitement and beginnings that smell like the outdoors.

your kiss, i am not sure i will ever forget, not by tomorrow, not in ten years time, not ever.

you think i am silly, don't you? but i did not ask for this.

i have not once cried to the universe to love more than i already can, she has just been overly generous with her emotions. i was born with my neck bound and my hands cold and it was the touch of human skin that warmed me right down to my middle; how could i have been expected to be anything other than desperate for affection?

i remember your touch.

that morning in my bed before you left,
the way your fingers found my cheeks and
stroked away any tears you found on my face.

i remember the navy shirt you were wearing
and how dark
the spots i made
from crying on your left shoulder
were.

i remember how it smelt
when i buried my face into the crook of your shoulder.
i remember hearing you close my front door
while i laid in my bed,
sobbing.

i cried so hard i think my legs
must have stopped working.

i couldn't have walked you out if i had wanted to.
if you had wanted me to.

i remember nothing of the next few weeks,
only how my heart ached.

oh,
how it ached.

tulips on my nightstand,
that i bought.
that i arranged.

i used to beg of you
to bring me home
anything
i could attend to.
anything
that was not
blonde hair strands on our unwashed pillow cases
or lipstick soaked collar bones.

if only you had given me kinder things to obsess over.

and i might not
have said
no,

and i might not
have pushed
you off of me,

but i said that it hurt
and i said that i didn't like it

and i think that should have been

enough.

i still buy oranges because they remind me of how it felt to love you. i eat them in the shower, naked and cross-legged. the flesh is sweet and the peel is wrinkled. i must have let them ripen for too long in my fruit bowl, afraid of finishing our enjoyment too soon, but i know time is not always kind to gentleness. you know this too, don't you? the juice drips down my palms to my elbows and there is nobody to kiss me clean. the rind lodges itself in the back of my throat and i do not dare to cough it back up. suffocating. terrified. exposed, embarrassed and sticky. this is how i loved you.

deluded- a guide to situationships

pick me apart
and show how the light shines through me.
you have stretched me
too thin.

i am ruined by you
and i bet you're damn proud of it.

deluded- a guide to situationships

i will waste away to love,
i promise you,
this person i have tried to enjoy,
is not a full meal.

they will never be enough for me,
not tomorrow,
not in a months' time,
not ever.
i will starve and shrivel and
plead for their crumbs.

they will withhold sustenance from me
because they will forever deem me
not worthy.

i am their midnight snack,
their secret tiptoe down to the fridge
in the middle of the night,
they are embarrassed to be crawling to me

and i will feed them,
while i am empty and hungry,
i will let them feast upon my body,
their appetite is ravenous for my skin.

i will find myself stuck between their teeth,
picked back out only to be swallowed again
and sealed inside of them among the other desperate, love-
hungry nobodies
who are also

begging for acceptance.

they kiss you on the forehead after sex
and then tell you they want nothing to do with you
the next day.

they text you non-stop for three weeks
and then ghost you,
after you finally agree
to send them pictures of you naked.

they date you for nearly two years
and then cheat on you, on a night out
because they got a little too drunk
and a little too carried away.

this is your modern romance
this is your twentieth-century love.

how disappointing.

they don't care about you,
they never have.
you just don't wanna admit it to yourself,
but you knew deep down
that it was never going to work out anyway,
didn't you?

you knew from the moment you met them,
but you buried your pretty little head into the sand
because you liked them,
you were hopeful,
but where has hope ever gotten you?

because now you are in your bed crying,
alone,
and he is out with whoever he wants to be out with,
whatever girl he's decided to spend his evening with,
not you-
never you.

it's not you he wants,
he's made that clear
and you've known from the beginning
he was always going to.
i'm so sorry
it fucking sucks
but i guess that's the price you pay for
love.

deluded- a guide to situationships

i didn't even date you,
but oh god,
do i miss you.

i mean,
christ!
i've gotten over two year relationships
easier than this!

and we only spent two months together
but i swear,
in my head,
those were the best two months
of my life.

i'm absolutely stuck,
thinking about
what could have been,
if we'd have had
more time,
more patience.

i know i could have loved you,
i know i could have.

and i know you could have loved me too.

some moments i knew i was (unfortunately) in love with you.

1- at your grandparents' house, meeting them for the first time and eating breakfast around their dining table- you cut into the bread we had made together and offered me the first slice of the loaf. you said you knew it was my favourite and i said *but i know it is yours too.* so we cut the slice into halves and ate it sat opposite each other, covered in apricot jam and smiles, blushing madly.

2- also at your grandparent's house, a few days into the trip and visiting the harbour together as we walked arm in arm- your grandparents showed us how they held hands in their own little peculiar way and we showed them how we held ours. you told me later you saw us in them and i could not breathe for the rest of the day.

3- writing you letter after letter and poem after poem while you were at sea- some hoping they would never be read, but others, pleading for you to like them. i wanted you to know i spent every waking moment thinking of you.

4- drunk and on holiday- you chasing me in the dark as i ran up the hill to our apartment. you telling me not to run because you loved me and because there was too much alcohol in your bloodstream to not. i did not say a single thing back, but i stopped and i let you grab my hand and i let you open our front door. i slept in your arms and mouthed the words back until cruel sleep took over my body and my mouth stopped working, but i said the words in my dream, all night long.

5- sat over a dinner table, in a restaurant we were too young and too poor to belong in- we were kids, drinking white wine and watching the world rotate together and you looked at me like i was all you could ever want. i excused myself to the toilet to cry with happiness, before returning and pouring you more wine. the sun went down in about as much time as it took for me to fall for you.

6- us in the ocean- my legs wrapped around your torso and salt water begging of me to close my eyes, but i couldn't. you looked so good in the sun, gloriously kind and mine and your mouth tasted delicious. my back to the shore, i saw you and nothing else. there were waves and feelings and not a single cloud in the sky that could stop me from wanting you.

7-the first moment i knew- before all of this other noise. watching your car drive away from me on the 20th of september 2020, knowing it would be months before i saw you again but thinking i would be okay with that, until i brushed hair off my face and tasted tears on my nose.

i did not know it was love, until it was.

it was not slow or expected or seen for what it was- i ignored every sign until i could not and by then i was nothing but a love-struck mess. the rest came easy, i saw love for what it was and i was not confused and i had moments of us to pin love to. once i knew that love was here existing happily, there was no ignoring it, there was only moment after moment of falling again and again and i would not change this for the world. not even if it meant you would come back to me.

they tell us how romantic it is
for love to not come to
just anyone.

they tell us love is supposed to be
difficult,
at the best of times.

they teach love as hair pulling,
eyelashes ripped out,
bodies broken and bruised.

they describe love as bending yourself
into a shape that someone else
might find more
attractive.

they make love out to be squeezing yourself
too small,
into a shape you do not belong in,
whether that is their arms
or their heart.

this must all be true,
this must be what love is,
they must have been correct all along,

because i suppose the alternative
is admitting the unhappy truth
that they *might not* have had
this love nonsense
entirely worked out.

the alternative is admitting
that the real love you want
could have always been easy,

that every love
you have had previously,
is not love.

and how heartbreaking is that?
to know what you have had,
is not even close.
not even a little bit.
not even at all.

to know what you grieved
was never worth grieving
in the first place.

i rewatched normal people
and crawled to the body of someone new.

i ate old pizza
 and drank flat coke.

i turned the heating all the way up
and i pretended i
didn't feel cold,
right down in my middle.

i smelt different aftershaves
on different skin and

i whittled holes in my heart
where your head once lay.

i was both everything and nothing
to nobody and everybody
and it was horrific.

this mangled mess of a human
only wanted you to
come back,

and oh, how it hurt
when you never did.

showering helps.

when the water touches my skin,
i stop belonging to you.
common knowledge is that
steamed up eyes cannot cry
and nothing has ever felt as good
as these fingers do
on this scalp.

when the water touches my skin
healing suddenly doesn't feel
like it would be all that difficult.
healing suddenly seems like
something i definitely could do.

when the water touches my skin,
my heart, for once,
does not feel so dirty.
i am clean and kind and warm
and i bathe the 'you' out of me
gently.

step 6

the end

i don't remember enough about us
to be able to daydream about you anymore.

it has been
months.

months of hurting and aching
and wondering if living like this
is really better than just dying.

months of not being to get out of bed
and holding my bladder until i get yet another uti.

months of eating shit food
followed by months of eating no food
followed by months of eating only rabbit food.

months of crying into my mother's lap
and being a burden to my friends
and a risk to myself.

months of hating every couple i see
holding hands in public.
wishing they would just stop rubbing their love
in my face
and wondering when, if ever,
i'd be able to hold someone else's
hand again.

months of
nothingness
and exhaustion and silence
and missing you.

months of it all.

and so many more months to go.

months to heal,
and to go out for dinners and
to take myself on solo cinema dates,
where i eat salted popcorn
until i feel sick.

months to recover
and to see the kindness in every sunrise.
to enjoy the colours and the stars and say goodbye
to the moon.

months to love someone new
and then someone more new
and then someone more new again.

love is not linear,
love is not always forever
and i have months to perfect
being okay with that.

i don't remember enough about us
to be able to daydream about you anymore.

and yes,
it is sad.
and yes,

part of me wishes
that i still could,

but i know that
time
only has my best interests
at heart.

i have had months to get over you.
i am getting there.
i am proud of my progress.

i have so many more months to go.

it was not love.
i did not burn and bury myself to be close to you
i was
always
at arm's length
and is love even possible at a distance?
can affection
be misconstrued for love
when i am not even sure
if you even knew how to spell my name correctly?

i am small
and unruly
and a cliche
and this is everything you hate about me.

i am the woman
that you will only ever refer to
as a girl
and that

is everything i hate about you.

i don't think right person wrong time really exists.

i think they didn't love you enough, or honestly, at all.

love is frustrating and difficult and always a little bit
inconvenient. love has never been anything but hard work
and effort.

the right person sees this, acknowledges how difficult your
relationship might be and chooses you anyway, because they
can't imagine living with the regret if they do not.

if they have not chosen you, it is not because it is the wrong
time, i think it is because they do not like you enough.

how exciting heartbreak is.

it might not feel like it in the moment,
but them leaving will be the best thing to have ever
happened to you.

if there may be one thing
that you have given me
during these months together,
if there may be one, single reasoning
for all of this pain that you have caused me,
it is nothing but
hope.

blind, stupid, unadulterated hope.

it is the knowledge that
if even mistreatment
can feel this good,
to be loved
must be the purest form of happiness
any of us could
ever aspire to achieve.

this hurt will fuel my excitement for love.
from this moment on
i vow to enjoy every little moment of love that
i am given.

how silly love is.

wretched and cruel and so warming.
you love wholly once
and then you never love quite the same
ever again.
usually.

you made the idea of love exciting again.
you made me wake up with my heart full of you
and hands yearning to match.
rain smelt better,
laundry day was less boring,
alcohol wasn't necessary.

i was drunk on you and you alone.

we need to talk about how cowardly
ghosting someone is.
how painful it is
to be left without an answer
or closure.

you can't just make someone like you
and then leave quietly,
it's not fair.
it's cruel.
and it's selfish.

just because you don't want to have
a difficult conversation,
doesn't meant you get to walk away
without one.

just
tell them
you're not interested.
just
be honest.

stop hurting other people
because you aren't ready to
admit how you feel.

untouched,
taste starved,
bruised and bitten tongue.
oh, how i have mistreated you.

i am sorry
i did not let you sit comfortably in my mouth,
i can only say that i began to be too afraid
of how you move
to let you touch the tips of my teeth
and be free.

you were the one thing in my life i could control
when he had taken hold of everything else.
my body was his,

at least my silence
was still mine.

do not frighten-
you are not in ownership of my heart anymore-
though i admit,
sometimes i do wish you were.

i am no longer yours,
you have never been mine

and that will be it.
that is our closure.
that is the end of everything we could have been,
but never quite were.

deluded- a guide to situationships

and so i wonder, if it wasn't for this skin and this body and these breasts, would i be happier? would i be someone with something to say and would somebody listen? would i enjoy meeting new people and not be so deathly afraid of how they grip my hand when they shake it? would i stop calling out for the 'warning signs' and mistaking kindness for manipulation and just take them as they come? would i be touched less? safer on buses? able to sleep without nightmares of being violated? would i be more myself if i did not have to worry about there being too much of me to be palatable? if it wasn't for this skin and this body and these breasts, if i had been born with a gender more likeable than my own, would i have been happier?

i want to write you poetry so gut-wrenchingly beautiful,
it makes you

g u l p .

choke on my words
and hate them
almost as much as you love them.

i want you to let the letters gouge out your eyes
and pin themselves
to the inside of your eyelids,
so that you may never sleep
without thinking of
me.

let me bury myself deep inside of you
and refuse to ever remove myself.
i will be there,
beneath the surface,
quietly writing,

and on days where the world is a little too
normal
and a little too
boring,
you will feel me underneath you skin,

an itch you cannot rid yourself of.
i am your worst nightmare transcribed,

i am healing
over and over and over

and then relapsing
again and again and again.

my poetry will ruin you,
if i do it right.
it will hold onto the sides of your head
and deafen you
to anything but me.

enjoy it,
i know i am going to.

oh i feel sorry for you
there are hundreds of men that i can find
exactly like you
but you'll not find a single woman like me.
not one to love you as kindly, as patiently,
not one who will do as much for you as i would have.
you'll never find someone as good to you as i was.
i pity you really
i wouldn't want to live a life without me.

you should know
that you are too vast
for the majority of men
to hold you kindly.

the moon is still the moon whether or not you are looking for it; breakfast still tastes delicious even if you eat it on a full stomach; hot showers can still be taken on summers days. my point is, among the madness and the nonsense and the impracticality of losing them, you are still you. you did not lose yourself too. sometimes it's okay to acknowledge that you have gone a little crazy, as long as you acknowledge that you are still you.

if there is anything i may teach you, my dear,
it is that you must not be ashamed
of how
and who
you love.
because oh my, do you love like i do.
you are cautious and overpowering
and your love is unstoppable.
you are dangerous,
in a good way i promise.
you are quill-written love letters,
ink stained fingertips,
bruised hearts
and hands longing for skin
that is not your own.
you are both afraid and impatient,
pleading and praying.
you are paper stretched too thin
that is still begging
to be written over.
oh my, you are hopeful.

and my dear,
you are music
made to be listened to,
in english fields
at 3:33am precisely.
you are daytime skies
and clouds pretty enough
to be watched
for hours.
you are linen curtains that let the light through,

the speckles of gold in eyes
that make lovers decide to love,
the color purple,
with no yellow mixed in.
you are perfect as you are,
complimentary color or not.
and i have never smelt you
but in my head i have imagined you
as smelling like an honest poem
i could only wish to write.
oh how i would love to be that true.
that transparent.
you are the hope i wish i could also be.

please do not lose that part of yourself to love.

i refuse to be cold. to have another human standing in front of me and do anything other than wrap my arms around them. i refuse to wear another short sleeve ever again- i have no need for clothes that do not give me warmth and allow for more room of my heart on my sleeve. i refuse to love sensibly, guardedly or pessimistically. i will be everything i wish i had been given as a child. i will be loud and unapologetic and kind. i will eat good food and drink good tea and trust good people and i will not regret a single second of it.

i promise myself,
with everything that i have in me,

i will not fall in love
with another man
who does not possess
the ability,
or the desperation,
of

loving

me

back.

you redownloaded the dating app you met them on. you ate
an orange again for the first time since the last night you
spent together. the juice dripped down your wrists and you
were okay with there being no one to kiss and lick you clean,
from finger to elbow. you listened to 'feel so close (radio
edit)' by calvin harris and you thought about how you
realised you were in love with them on that sweaty nightclub
dance floor abroad (it was far too soon into knowing them so
you shut your mouth, but smiled the entire night). you
thought about how they probably don't even know the
importance of that song to you. you drank red wine and
kissed some stranger with a shitty moustache in the bar you
both always talked about trying out next weekend. you
redecorated. you painted every wall in your bedroom,
changed the bedding twice and filled their now empty
drawers with stupid impulse purchases, hoping if you could
scrub clean this room, if you could rid this space of anything
relating to them, then you might be able to close your eyes
without your dreams being filled with them.

it worked.

you hated that it worked.

but it worked, nonetheless.

and then suddenly it was sunday. and life was streaming in
through the linen curtains, that cost far too much money for
such little darkness. you drank in the sun before leaving your
bed and you let your newish purple bedsheets hold you
kindly. you rolled over and smelt half dried lavender and
honeysuckle and happiness. you crossed your legs and your
heart and your fingers and you wished for some sadness to

find you, for something comforting, like heartbreak. but it could not. on this sunday morning. sadness could not find its way through this sun and these walls and this home.

yes, they left. yes, it broke you. yes, you thought it would last forever. but it didn't. you are here now, my child. you are alive and your chest is rising and your toes are wriggling and you cannot remember ever feeling angry at yourself for healing this nicely. you are whole and you always have been, because a heartbreak and a silly person cannot change that. you are enough and loving and loved and deserving and you know this now. if these months have taught you anything, it is that you know there is no one who can complete or ruin you.

no one, and i mean no one, has that power.

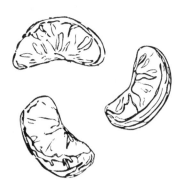

THE END

ACKNOWLEDGEMENTS

thank you to every single person who has helped bring this book to life and to the people who brought me back to life.

to ang, a dear friend/editor/videographer/graphic designer/all around delight. you mean more to me than you'll ever know, and your friendship brings me a ridiculous amount of happiness.

to sam and laura, the most talented women whom i am forever thankful to have met and worked with. you took my visions and breathed life into them. this book cover and these illustrations are everything i have ever imagined them to be and more.

to my mum, who is always my loudest cheerleader. thank you for never doubting me and my work. i'm so lucky to have such an inspirational woman as a role-model.

to my readers and my followers, thank you for being you, for being so kind and supportive and always allowing me to do what i love. writing poetry has saved me countless times. i extend my largest thank you to you, for given me a reason to keep writing.

and to every situationship, to every not-quite-relationship, to every person i have dated who pretended to be one of the good one's, you get no thank you. you get, quite frankly, the largest fuck you in existence. i hope you hated this book and i hope you question if every poem is about you.

sleep well, my darlings, speak soon. x

SAMAMTHA SANDERSON-MARSHALL
- book cover artist

with over 50 book covers designed, sam is a well established, gorgeously talented graphic designer and book cover artist, she has a 1st class degree in graphic design and uses a plethora of artistic skills to create each book cover. sam adores collaborating with various written genres and authors, and has works held in the british national library and the vaults of cambridge and oxford universities. she was shortlisted for the 2022 brighton fringe.

sam lives in merseyside in the uk, with her two cats and a puppy, who she refers to as more difficult to parent than her kids. sam generally spends her days drinking ridiculous amounts of black coffee, and listening to 90s hip hop while she draws in her almost entirely black studio.

www.smashdesigns.co.uk
@smashdesignsbooks on instagram

LAURA MARTIN
- internal illustrations

laura is passionate graphic designer, who thrives on bringing creative visions to life through visual storytelling. with a keen eye for detail and a love for aesthetics, she specializes in creating captivating designs that leave a lasting impression. find her on instagram or online to discuss bringing your design project to life!

www.fromthehammock.ca
@fromthehammock on instagram

ABOUT THE AUTHOR

isabella dorta is the four time, best selling author of *how sunflowers bloom under moonlight.* she self published her first book on february 14th 2022. as a true victim of heartbreak and love, her poetry is birthed from real life and proudly tells isabella's story.

isabella grew up in reading, with her mum and her brother, but now lives just outside of bath, on an old, abandoned farm, in the middle of nowhere. she has three cats, far too many house plants and describes herself as 'more a cliche than [she] could have ever hoped to be'.

known for reading her poetry aloud on social media, isabella refers to herself not as a poet, but as a young woman who just feels things 'a little too ferociously'. she posted her first poem online in may of 2021 and has since built a loving community of followers, who have given isabella a platform to continue writing/performing her poetry.

www.isabelladortapoetry.com
find isabella on tiktok and instagram
@isabelladortapoetry444

Printed in Great Britain
by Amazon

38269090R00108